To

_____

From

_____

Date

_____

Summerside Press™
Minneapolis 55378
www.summersidepress.com

60 Promises to Pray for Your Marriage
© 2012 Gwen Ford Faulkenberry

ISBN 978-1-60936-198-3

Designed by Koechel Peterson & Associates
Interior design and typesetting by Jeff Jansen | www.aestheticsoup.net

Summerside Press™ is an inspirational publisher offering fresh, irresistible books to uplift the heart and engage the mind.

Printed in China.

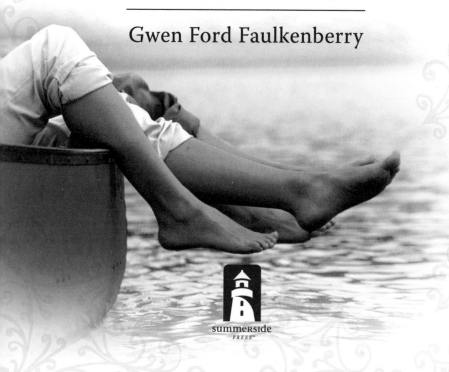

Promises
to Pray
for your marriage

Gwen Ford Faulkenberry

summerside
PRESS™

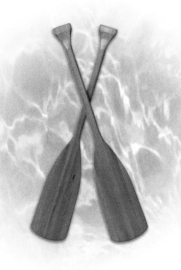

Dedicated to
Stone Faulkenberry:
my husband, my lover,
and my best friend.

Contents

Section
1

The Promise of Blessing

I will bless you...
and you will be a blessing.

GENESIS 12:2

The Bible is full of promises. Because God always keeps His promises, we can cling to them and claim them over our marriages. One of the greatest promises He makes is that He will bless us.

The Lord delights in blessing His people. As His children, we live in the atmosphere of His blessing. It is the air we breathe. There is never a moment in our lives—or our marriages—that escapes His notice. Never a time He's not seeking to bless us. There will never be a moment so good that His blessing can't make it better. There will also never be a moment so difficult His blessing can't help.

Because of how God blesses us, we become bearers of His blessing in the lives of others. He created the marriage relationship with enormous potential for blessing. Husbands and wives are gifted with great power to bless one another. And as couples dedicated to the Lord, we can offer a unique blessing to our families, friends, community, and the entire world.

The Blessing of the Lord

I the LORD will be their God....
I will bless them....
There will be showers of blessing.

EZEKIEL 34:24, 26

Dear Father, Your Word promises that You will bless us. Thank You that we can trust You to do what You say. We claim the promise of blessing today for our marriage. We pray that You would pour out Your blessing like fresh rain. We thirst for You. Bring the showers we need.

We know that You see us right where we are and You know our circumstances. Nothing is hidden from You. You know our strengths, our weaknesses, our dreams, and our regrets. You know how desperately our marriage needs Your blessing in order to grow and thrive. It's our hearts' desire that we, as a couple, can be the beautiful force for good You intended us to be in the world. Help us become that.

You know the areas with which we are struggling right now. We pray Your blessing into those areas. Let Your light shine into the dark places between us that we might find the way to new life. Lord, release us from our bondages. Make clear the pathway out of our struggles and into Your peace.

Thank You for the hope of Your blessing. In Your hands our marriage can be a thing of joy and purpose, a beacon of overcoming life. In Your hands we are destined for beauty, not ashes. You are shaping us into vessels of honor.

This day may Your blessing fall fresh on us, nourishing and bringing to fruition the work You started in us the day we said "I do."

The Blessing of Salvation

For God so loved the world that he gave his one and only Son, that whoever believes in him shall not perish but have eternal life.

JOHN 3:16

Thank You, God, for the promise of Your salvation. Thank You for the gift You gave us when You sent Your Son into the world. Reaffirming our belief in Jesus, we pray that You would restore to us the joy of Your salvation.

What a vast, immeasurable gift it is. Thank You for the security of eternal life, for the assurance that heaven is our future home. Thank You also that through Jesus the kingdom of heaven is here now for us to participate in and enjoy.

We pray the blessings of the kingdom over our marriage today. Show us how to work out our salvation as we grow closer to one another and to You. Where there is wrong in our relationship, make it right. Where there is pride in our lives, bring us to brokenness. Where there is strife between us, let there be peace. Where there is misunderstanding, help us find clarity. Where there is dishonesty in our communication, bring forth Your truth and let it reign in our home.

Where there is unforgiveness, help us to forgive as Jesus does. Where there is anger, soften our hearts. Where there are unmet expectations, let there be acceptance. Let any disrespect be replaced with honor—honor for You first, and then one another.

You have saved us. Continue saving us from a life of mediocrity. Help us to live in this world every day in the light of Your salvation...as citizens of a spiritual country, children of the one true King.

The Blessing of Work

Let the beauty of the LORD our God be upon us, and establish the work of our hands for us; yes, establish the work of our hands.

PSALM 90:17 NKJV

Oh, Lord, what a comfort it is to know that You call us to our work and lead us in it.

Thank You that You have put us together in marriage to be a light in the world and given us a purpose for the work of our hands. We pray today that Your beauty would be upon us, and that You would bless the work You have called us to do. Help us remember today that You have called us to help each other fulfill that calling. Let all of our work be as unto You, and not just to please others or ourselves.

We pray, Father, that You would help us to be lights for You in our workplaces. Lead us to others who need to see Jesus. Give us clear vision, that we may open the eyes of those who are blind. Help us not to shy away from those in darkness, but to seek them out and offer the light of life.

Because You have called us, our work is so much more than just a daily grind, or even a quest for earthly success. We are Yours. And that means that wherever we are, and especially in the work You call us to, we are Your ambassadors. May others see Jesus in the quality of our work, and in the attitudes of our hearts. Bless the work we do, Lord, that we might bring honor and glory to Your name.

The Blessing of His Power

But you will receive power when the Holy Spirit comes on you, and you will be my witnesses in Jerusalem, and in all Judea and Samaria, and to the ends of the earth.

Acts 1:8

Jesus, thank You that You have not called us to witness for You without also supplying the power to fulfill that calling. We admit that sometimes we feel overwhelmed by the thought of being Your witness in our marriage, not to mention our community and the "ends of the earth." While sometimes it would be easier to focus on the outside world and the endless opportunities it holds for being Your witness, we know Your perfect order of things is that we get it right at home first. That can be so challenging!

And yet, You have promised us the power we need through the Holy Spirit. We cling to that promise today. Come and fill us with Your power. It is in You, by You, and through You that we will fulfill the promises in our marriage.

By Your power, Jesus, we choose to lay down our lives and follow You. By Your power, we choose to see our marriage as an opportunity to serve. By Your power, we will see as You see and love as You love. We can be faithful to the calling of God not because of ourselves, and not because of how another person reacts or treats us, but because of the power that lives in us. If we have to call on Your power a thousand times today, we will, in order to be Your witness. Thank You that Your power is enough to keep us faithful through every moment of this day—and every day.

The Blessing of Others

I will bless you; I will make your name great, and you will be a blessing.

Genesis 12:2

Thank You, Father, that You have blessed our marriage. We are amazed daily with the surprise of Your care for us, how You build us up, and how You protect our reputations individually and as a couple. Oh, Lord, how awesome Your blessings are. Help us to rejoice as we count each one. You have promised that You will bless us and that we will in turn bless others. We put our faith in that promise today.

Father, help us to find ways to bless those around us according to Your will and pleasure. Use our marriage as a safe place for those who need refuge. Give us provision so we may provide for those who don't have enough. Bless us with Your wisdom and understanding that we may guide and advise those seeking Your path. Pour out Your compassion on us so that it spills over to our friends and family just when they need it. Bless us so we can keep on blessing and blessing.

Every blessing, every gift, every breath comes from You, Father. Our marriage is built upon those blessings. We pray that You will continue to find favor in us, continue to connect our name with Yours, continue to use us and our marriage to fulfill Your plan. Open our hearts to others and show us how to share Your blessings.

The Blessing of His Presence

You have made known to me the path of life; you will fill me with joy in your presence, with eternal pleasures at your right hand.

PSALM 16:11

Oh, Lord, how good it is to be in Your presence. That is the best blessing of all—not even all of the wonderful things You give us, but You. Yourself. That You are with us.

Thank You that You are present in our marriage. Thank You that You never leave us, but You are always there, gently guiding us along the path of life. Help us to listen to Your voice and to follow You. You give us so many pleasures, so many blessings. We know that all good things flow into our lives from Your hand.

Today, we thank You for our marriage. Thank You that You have given us each other to live with, learn from, and serve. Thank You for what You are doing in our lives both individually and as a couple. Thank You that You are always working out Your will in us. We pray that we would never be stubborn and work against You, but that we would be like pliable clay in Your able hands.

Teach us, today, to live in Your presence; to look for You in all things that affect our marriage, big and small. We know that in every moment You seek an entrance to our hearts. May we fling open the doors and welcome You in. May Your presence be our joy, our honor. And through our marriage, may others sense Your presence and be drawn to the beauty and blessing of You.

Section
2

The Promise of His Guidance

*When he, the Spirit of truth, comes, he
will guide you into all truth.... He will
bring glory to me by taking from what is
mine and making it known to you.*

JOHN 16:13–14

Someone once said, "Without the Spirit, anything we do is meaningless." This statement includes anything we do in marriage. All of our seeking, all of our striving, all of our efforts really come to nothing without the Lord's guidance in our lives.

However, with His guidance, even the smallest task can be infused with purpose and meaning. And, even the largest goal can be accomplished because of His power. We don't have to live mundane lives because He is in the details. We don't have to live in defeat because He is big enough to give us victory over any problem. And we don't have to force anything in our marriage because He makes the way clear for us; He makes the path smooth.

The Holy Spirit's function is to bring glory to Jesus by guiding us in God's truth. He is our guide, our helper, our comforter, our friend. He's a marriage counselor who is there every moment to gently offer advice if we will listen, and His advice never fails, because He is the Spirit of truth.

Our Counselor

The Counselor,
the Holy Spirit,
whom the Father
will send in my name,
will teach you all things
and will remind you
of everything
I have said to you.

JOHN 14:26

Father, thank You for sending Your Holy Spirit into the world. Thank You that because of Him we are not alone in our marriage, but we have a friend who walks beside us, guiding us and teaching us and reminding us of You. We come to You now and ask You to fill us with Your Spirit, that we may walk in Your truth and bring glory and honor to Jesus through our marriage.

May Your Spirit rest upon us today. Reveal Jesus to us, that we may know Him better. Remind us of who He has been to us in the past, where He has taken us, what He has spoken to our hearts, the life He has given us. Strengthen us as we remember past blessings, past victories, past promises He has fulfilled. We look to You also for new teaching. Give us new direction in our marriage as we seek to go deeper with You. Open our hearts to listen to Your voice and receive Your instruction. We know that what You have to say to us is true and right, and brings freedom in our lives.

You are the great Counselor. Please help us to face the truth about the issues we are dealing with in our marriage. We know You have provided a way out of struggle and into Your peace. Set our feet on the right path and show us the way to peace with one another and with God, in all things big and small.

The Gift of the Spirit

Repent and be baptized, every one of you, in the name of Jesus Christ for the forgiveness of your sins. And you will receive the gift of the Holy Spirit. The promise is for you and your children.

Acts 2:38–39

Lord, we praise You today for the promise of Your presence in our marriage. Sometimes it is easy to think that the gift of Your presence is for other people, people who are more spiritual than we are. But Your Word says You will be with us. You have called us and we are Your children. Like salvation, the work of the Spirit in our lives—Your presence—is not something we earn, but a gift You freely give us. We accept the gift of Your presence into our lives—and into our marriage—right now.

Come, Lord, and work in our marriage. Move among us; fill us; renew us. We are keenly aware that we need You in our lives. It is so easy to get caught up in the "stuff" of life—the things we have to do to keep going—that sometimes we ignore You. We are sorry for that. Please forgive us. We don't want to hinder Your work in our lives. We want You to freely flow through us, having Your perfect way in our marriage. We realize that Your work in us may not look the same as it does in other people. We invite You to change our lives, to bring glory to Jesus through us. May we never limit Your creativity or Your power.

Give us ears to listen and the courage to follow wherever You lead. We look forward to having Your presence with us today.

Our Intercessor

We do not know what we ought to pray for, but the Spirit himself intercedes for us through wordless groans. And he who searches our hearts knows the mind of the Spirit, because the Spirit intercedes for God's people in accordance with the will of God.

ROMANS 8:26–27

Dear Father, as we come before You today, we don't even know how to pray for our marriage. We long for Your Spirit to descend on us, to change us, to take our weaknesses and make us strong. But sometimes the list seems so long we don't know where to start. And sometimes we sense there are things below the surface that we can't even see about ourselves. We're crying out for Your mercy even to know how to pray.

Thank You, Father, that we can rely on You. Thank You that You see all things—even things that are buried in the subconscious, things we don't know and cannot discern. Thank You that You are not limited to words, but that You search our hearts and know everything. Please guide us even in the things we are not able to express. Help us choose the right words, that we may find the grace of God.

What a comfort it is to know that the Holy Spirit intercedes for us. That even the deep mysteries are not hidden from You. That all aspects of our marriage are brought before You. That there is no weakness of ours that can limit the power of prayer, because we can pray in Your power. As we listen and wait for You, we place our marriage into Your hands. We trust the Spirit to intercede for us in accordance with God's perfect will.

God Knows the Plans

"For I know the plans I have for you," declares the LORD, *"plans to prosper you and not to harm you, plans to give you hope and a future."*

JEREMIAH 29:11

Father, thank You that You have amazing things prepared for our marriage, things no eye has seen, nor ear heard, nor mind conceived. Thank You that You are always working out Your will in us, bringing Your plans to completion, conforming us to the likeness of Your Son. And thank You that by Your Holy Spirit we can participate in Your divine plans.

We pray that You will reveal Your purposes and plans to us. Thank You that You have a future worked out for us. It dazzles us to think that You know the deep things of God, that nothing is hidden from You, and that You gently guide our marriage according to that knowledge. May we be so close to You, so in tune with Your Spirit, that we too can know the deep things of God and live them out in our marriage.

We're excited and humbled that You would promise beautiful things for our lives, Lord. We pray You would help us to cling to that blessed hope in our marriage, and not allow temporary circumstances to get us down. Reveal truths to us that cannot be seen with our eyes or heard with our ears. Quicken our hearts to keep in step with the plans of Your Spirit. And give us the courage to follow your plans for our future and trust that they will always be for our good.

Choices

Whether you turn to the right or to the left, your ears will hear a voice behind you, saying, "This is the way; walk in it."

Isaiah 30:21

How wonderful are Your promises to us, oh, God. Marvelous are Your ways. You have shown us the pathway to peace, the way to live the best life here on earth, and You have also provided the means, the strength, the power to choose that life. Because of You, our life together can be a journey in overcoming, a joyous victory.

We pray Your blessing over our marriage and claim Your power today. By Your Spirit we choose Your path in all of our interactions. We invite You to take charge of our day and guide our choices.

With Your help, we choose to speak loving words instead of speaking unkindly. We choose to have a gentle touch. We choose to honor our marriage partner above others, and to put our marriage before more trivial pursuits. We choose unselfishness over our own desires, our own rights. We choose to serve rather than expecting to be served. We choose to look out for one another's good rather than focusing only on selfish desires in our relationship. We choose patience. We choose discipline and self-control.

Father, we know that without a change of heart these choices are behavioral, and only temporary. But today we are choosing to be transformed on the inside by the power of Your Spirit. Let our behavior flow out of soft and yielded hearts. Truly change us, that we may live by the Spirit every day, no longer following a sinful path, but bringing glory to Jesus.

Marked

You also were included in Christ when you heard the word of truth, the gospel of your salvation. Having believed, you were marked in him with a seal, the promised Holy Spirit.

EPHESIANS 1:13

Thank You, Lord, that we have a mark that shows we belong to You. When we heard the gospel and believed in Jesus, You sealed our relationship with the Holy Spirit, a sign that we are Yours. Just like a wedding ring. As a couple we exchanged rings to show that we belong to one another and that everything we have and are belongs to the other, forever. It's a promise. A sacred vow.

Thank You, Father, for the promise that You placed on us with the seal of Your Spirit. In our marriage, we pray that You will pour out the bounty of that promise. We want our lives to reveal Your mark—Your love, Your power, Your provision, Your joy—all that You promised. We want an abundant life in Jesus. Thank You for giving us the opportunity as a couple to walk with You and know You and enjoy Your presence. We bind ourselves to You forever and want the evidence of that to be visible in our lives. Thank You that You hold nothing back from us.

We offer our marriage to You. Keeping nothing in reserve, we give You everything we are, including our weaknesses. May our marriage, by being marked by You, become something beautiful, to the praise of Your glory. Thank You that You keep Your vows and that You never leave us. May Your Spirit help us to be more like You as we seek to keep our vows to each other.

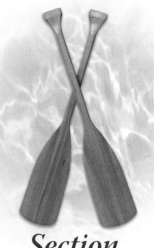

Section
3

The Promise of Intimacy

Now this is eternal life:
that they may know you, the only true God,
and Jesus Christ, whom you have sent.

JOHN 17:3

Intimacy—spiritual and physical oneness—is a huge need in marriage. The absence of intimacy between spouses can be damaging, while its presence is a great blessing from God. He designed us to be intimate with one another. And as in everything else, He supplies all we need for that to happen.

The deepest intimacy with our spouses is made possible only through intimacy with God. John 17:3 says that eternal life is to know Him. The word for know there is not a casual knowing. It's not knowing as we know an acquaintance, or even a good friend. It means to know intimately. Like a husband and wife. In other words, the King stepped out of His castle and into the fabric of our lives. He offers Himself to us as a bridegroom—that we may know Him intimately. Everything He has, everything He is, He shares with us.

In marriage, we are to follow His example and share ourselves intimately with our spouses—physically, spiritually, and mentally. When we call on God to guide us, we find that intimacy with Him and with each other can soar to new heights.

God with Us

The virgin will be with child and will give birth to a son, and they will call him "Immanuel"—which means, "God with us."

Matthew 1:23

Thank You, Jesus, that You are with us. That we can live in Your presence as a daily reality. You are not some far-off deity who cannot be reached. You are always there for us, always with us as our brother and our friend, even though You are our King.

We praise You today as our God and King. You are Lord of everything—Lord over all of creation, and Lord over every detail that concerns us. Thank You that You are in control and You care about our marriage.

We acknowledge You as Lord over our marriage. Jesus, our Immanuel, come and be with us in our home. May Your presence be the focus of every meal, every conversation, every moment. May we welcome You as our honored guest.

How we need You to be with us, Jesus. We are dependant on You for every breath. As we walk through this day, hold our hands, keep us together in Your Spirit. Let the words of our mouths and the meditations of our hearts be acceptable in Your sight. Give us a heart like Yours toward each other and bind us together in love. We desire to know You intimately, so You can help us to know each other intimately.

As You walk with us, Jesus, help us to become more like You. Shape us into Your image that we may see with Your eyes, love as You love, live as You would have us live. Come, be with us, Jesus, and establish our marriage into a union that brings glory to You.

A Helper

The LORD God said, "It is not good for the man to be alone. I will make a helper suitable for him."

GENESIS 2:18

Oh, Lord, how we thank You for the gift of a helper. In Your wisdom You saw that it's not good for us to go through life alone, and You provided exactly what we need in one another. Help us today to remember that. Help us look to each other—and each other only—for that intimate relationship You provided in marriage. May there be no lonely places between us.

Husband: Thank You for my wife, my bride. My heart is to love her as You love the Church, Jesus, and daily to give myself up for her needs. I pray that You will show me ways I can be a helper to her—around the house, in big and small things, in things that are outward and things of the inner life. May I live with her in an understanding way, leading as a servant, and cherishing her as the gift she is from You.

Wife: Thank You, Lord, for my husband. Thank You for all of the good things he is in my life. My desire is to be a helper and an encourager to him. A strengthening support. A lover and a friend. Help me to always be respectful toward him and to build him up, never tear him down. May I be a wife who brings joy to his heart and to Yours.

One Flesh

After all, no one ever hated his own body, but he feeds and cares for it, just as Christ does the church—for we are members of His body. "For this reason a man will leave his father and mother and be united to his wife, and the two will become one flesh."

Ephesians 5:29–31

One flesh. God, this is one of Your divine mysteries. It's something we can't comprehend, and yet it is something You allow us to enjoy—a miracle in which You invite us to participate. Wow.

Sometimes it's easy to think of "one flesh" as being only about physical intimacy, but today we want to pray the promise of intimacy over our marriage in a different way. Like the verse says, we pray that we would begin to love one another as we love our own bodies. To truly see each other beyond the surface and seek to understand how it feels to live in our spouse's skin. Make us so close in spirit that we anticipate each other's needs even as we anticipate the needs of our own bodies, like hunger, thirst, warmth, and rest. Help us provide those things to one another insofar as we are able, and when it is beyond us, help us lead the other to You—the Source with no limits.

May we care for one another and feed one another, not only physically, but spiritually as well. May we become one in body and in spirit. May we nurture life and health in our marriage so our home will thrive.

Lovers

I belong to my lover and his desire is for me.... At our door is every delicacy, both new and old.

<small>Song of Solomon 7:10, 13</small>

Father, You are an amazing God. You know us inside and out. Not only did You give us marriage so that we would have a helper to walk beside us in life, but You also intended us for physical pleasure. Thank You for the gift of sex—and for making it a holy, spiritual experience in marriage. An opportunity to give to one another and to receive the blessing of true oneness through You.

Help us, Father, as individuals, to be sensitive to one another's sexual needs. Help us to be understanding, gentle, and kind. It seems that in this area, as in others, there is so much opportunity for the enemy to attack us. We pray Your protection over our marriage. Help us to always be faithful to one another both physically and mentally. With our eyes and our minds as well as our hearts. We claim Your promise of oneness and Your blessing over our marriage bed today.

Father, You know any obstacles to physical intimacy we may have, from the past or the present. By Your power help us to overcome those. Let Your love cover our imperfections. Let Your grace surround us that we might freely extend it to one another. We long to enjoy the deep fulfillment You can give us even in this physical area. Thank You for my lover, and that You are the Lover of our souls.

Sacred Intimacy

Honor marriage, and guard the sacredness of sexual intimacy between wife and husband.

HEBREWS 13:4 MSG

Marriage is lived so closely, so intimately. It is the ultimate sharing of oneself. Lord, help us to honor the sacredness of our relationship in all areas: our hearts, our minds, our emotions, our spirits, our bodies. Keep us true to each other and to our marriage vows.

Lord, purity is not only about protecting sexual intimacy—although that is a major component. It is about guarding our feelings for each other and not letting others intrude. It is about turning away from immoral photos, shows, or websites, keeping the focus on our spouse. It is about seeing our relationship as something sacred, something that goes beyond how we feel, see, or experience. It is about a choice to love with great passion on every level. Lord, only through You can we love like that. Protect the intimacy we have as a couple and keep it pure. Make it more real and more precious every single day.

Help us to open ourselves to each other, to be willing to share every corner of our beings with each other. Sometimes, Lord, it is tempting to hide things, to put on a mask, or to hold back. Let us not. True intimacy requires true openness with each other. Lord, we trust You to move us into a sacredness of intimacy that makes openness like that possible. Bless our marriage with frankness, understanding, and an intimacy that honors You.

Communication

Always be humble and gentle. Be patient with each other, making allowance for each other's faults because of your love. Make every effort to keep yourselves united in the Spirit, binding yourselves together with peace.

EPHESIANS 4:2–3 NLT

Thank You, God, for sending Jesus to be the Light of the world. Because of Him we can walk in the light and not be overcome by darkness in our lives or in our marriage. Thank You for the communication we have with You and with one another. Use it to light the way for understanding in our marriage.

We pray today that You will bring us into deeper fellowship as husband and wife in our marriage, and in our relationship with You. Help us, through fellowship with You, to be totally open and honest with one another. When problems arise, give us the courage to talk them through, to be gentle and humble. Give us patience to discover the needs and wants we each have in order to build intimacy between us. Help us to make every effort to communicate fully and peacefully.

Our desire, God, is that our marriage be totally filled with Your light. We pray that we would walk together in step with You, that You would cast out any fear that inhibits our communication with one another or with You. Where Your light is, darkness has no power. We pray Your promise of fellowship over our marriage today. We pray that we will always pursue open communication with You and that we may enjoy more and more fellowship with one another as we bind ourselves together in peace.

Community

Where two or three come together in my name, there am I with them.

Matthew 18:20

Dearest Jesus, I praise You for the promise that You are with us—even two or three of us—when we gather in Your name. As we bow before You, we claim that promise for our marriage. Be with us, always. We need You every moment, every hour. Without You we are nothing.

We pray today that as You lead us in oneness with each another, You also will lead us into fellowship with other believers.

We recognize that need in our lives. Help us look for opportunities to gather with people in community. Lead us to others whose lives You want us to touch—to opportunities where You want us to invest ourselves. Give us people who can help us to grow and whom we can trust to walk with us in our life journey.

Help us to be patient and compassionate toward everyone. Help us not to judge. Guard us against hidden prejudices we may not even know we have. Stretch us and shape us to conform to Your image in all things—especially as we seek spiritual intimacy with other believers.

Let us see others as You see them, looking at the heart rather than anything outward. Open our minds and our spirits to Your leading, that we may form friendships and alliances that glorify You. We know We know You give only good gifts and we want to experience all You have for us as we gather together with Your people in Your presence.

Section
4

The Promise of Peace

Peace I leave with you; my peace I give you.
I do not give to you as the world gives.
Do not let your hearts be troubled
and do not be afraid.

John 14:27

Jesus—Himself—is our peace. He provided the way for us to make peace with God. He is also the way for us to find peace with ourselves and to live in peace with others. Because of Jesus, we can have peace no matter what our circumstances. He doesn't change. His peace is like a still, clear pool of water that cannot be disturbed by any force or outward stirring. It is always there for us, a pure and living source that never runs dry.

The peace that Jesus gives us is not dependant on our performance. Unlike the way of the world, He does not give peace to us because we earn it. His peace is also something no person—nor any circumstance—can ever take away. On the days that our relationships are strained, our nerves stretched, or our behavior regretful, peace is still available to us and for us to extend to our spouse.

His desire for us as individuals and in marriage is always peace. Peace is the direction He wants to lead us, and it is the evidence of His presence in our lives. He came in peace so that our hearts could be free of trouble, our spirits free of fear, and our marriages free of strife.

The Blessing of Peace

The LORD bless you and keep you; the LORD make his face shine upon you and be gracious to you; the LORD turn his face toward you and give you peace.

NUMBERS 6:24-26

Lord, Your Word promises the blessing of Your peace over Your people. We call to You now, as Your children, and pray this promise over our marriage. Please bless and keep us. Make Your face to shine upon us. Turn Your face toward us, be gracious to us, and give us peace. Thank You for putting Your name on us; thank You that You bless us with peace.

Lord, You know what is going on in our lives and all of the things that threaten our peacefulness. We know that You reign over all of those things and that You can help us through them. Help us to abide in Your peace. Help us to dig deep and allow the roots of our marriage to grow further and further into Your love, that we may rest in Your peace.

We look to You today for peace in our marriage. We choose You over our own resources, which in reality are so limited. We choose You and Your promise of peace over anything we may say, feel, or do. Your peace reigns over how anyone may treat us, any news we may receive. Your peace reigns even over our own poor judgments or bad decisions or angry retorts. Today is a new day. A day for peace. May we walk in Your peace—moment by moment—through this whole day. And may our marriage be a reflection of Your peace.

Peace with God's Will

Therefore, since we have been justified through faith, we have peace with God through our Lord Jesus Christ, through whom we have gained access by faith into this grace in which we now stand.

ROMANS 5:1–2

Jesus, thank You so much for coming and giving Your life that through You we may be at peace with God. We often want to wrestle with Your direction, or Your timing, but in our hearts we know that Your will is perfect. Peace comes when we surrender completely to You. Please help us to do that today. We are laying down our will and accepting Yours.

Today, we pray for an extra measure of Your peace in our hearts that we may be peace-bringers in our marriage. There are areas we need to address in order for Your peace to flow between us and through us. Give us Your Spirit, Jesus. Give us wisdom. Help us to gently and humbly share with each other and also help us to be open, to agree with one another and with You. We know this is Your heart for us. This is part of what it means to live life to the full.

We thank You again, Jesus, for the ultimate peace You have available for our marriage. Our desire is that our relationship would be a journey through life in day-to-day peace, that we would never step outside of Your will. Show us how to live in a way that pleases You. Let Your peace rest upon our marriage.

Peace Within

You will keep in perfect peace him whose mind is steadfast, because he trusts in you. Trust in the LORD forever, for the LORD, the LORD, is the Rock eternal.

ISAIAH 26:3–4

Father, You know us. You know our marriage, our lives. You know everything about us. We admit that we are struggling today. "Peace" seems like an elusive concept. We long for it. It's like a beautiful butterfly we keep chasing, yet it stays just out of our reach.

We confess our fretfulness to You today. You came to give us victory over worry and still here we are, allowing worry to consume us and steal our peace. Forgive us, Lord. Cleanse our hearts of worry and replace it with Your peace. Because of You, we know that we can have peace in any circumstance. We're choosing to turn away from worry and to walk in the other direction—toward Your peace.

Lord, we trust You with our marriage. We trust You with one another, and with all of the things that are stressful right now. All of the things we don't understand. You are bigger than these things, bigger than our marriage, bigger than anything that is going on in our marriage. Your peace is great enough to cover us. We give You all of our worries, including our finances, health, our families—everything.

Oh, Lord, You truly are the Rock eternal. We cling to the promise that nothing can change You. You will provide perfect peace within us. As we come to You in prayer, as we focus our thoughts on You, may Your peace rest on us like a butterfly coming to rest on our shoulders.

Peace with One Another

Be kind to each other, tenderhearted, forgiving one another, just as God through Christ has forgiven you.

EPHESIANS 4:32 NLT

Dear Father, thank You that peace in our marriage is possible through Your Son. Because of Jesus we don't have to live selfish lives, demanding our own rights. He has shown us a better way—a higher way. We know everyone has disagreements and we ask You to teach us how to walk through them calmly, keeping peace as our goal. We want to choose the higher way, the forgiving way.

You have promised that "peacemakers" will be called Your children. Oh, how we want to bring joy to Your heart as Your children. Lord, by Your Spirit transform us into peacemakers and our marriage into an example of Your peace.

We know to be peacemakers we must forgive, no matter what. By Your power we choose forgiveness. Help us in our marriage to show the same mercy that has been given to us by Jesus. We give our disappointment to You. We trust You to help us deal with it so that we can be free with no grudges held between us.

Guard our tongues, Father. May our words be seasoned with kindness, to preserve our relationship and not to wound. Give us self-control that we would not stir up trouble but would offer forgiveness. Help us have soft voices that turn away wrath and make peace, rather than contributing to strife.

Father, we recognize that we cannot force tranquility into our marriage. But we can be at peace with You, and we can be vessels of Your peace to each other. Help us to always strive for peace.

Agree in Peace

Then make me truly happy by agreeing wholeheartedly with each other, loving one another, and working together with one mind and purpose.

<small>PHILIPPIANS 2:2 NLT</small>

Dear heavenly Father, thank You for letting us find each other. You took two totally different people and blended us into one family. We are so grateful for Your work in our marriage, for showing us how to make decisions as one when we are two separate people.

Father, as You know, we don't always agree on our goals, our decisions, or even where to go for dinner. Sometimes we are stressed out and peace seems impossible. But You say in Your Word that nothing is impossible with You. We may disagree, but You have a way of bringing us together. Lord, guide our discussions, help us focus on working together with the single purpose of pleasing You. Guard our words to each other. Help us to consider the other's feelings and reasoning as we work and plan together.

Help us to come to agreement in peace, Father. We see married couples fighting against each other, worried about their selfish desires. We want to love each other wholeheartedly, listen attentively, and make decisions calmly. Fill us with Your peace as we walk together toward our future, putting our spouse's needs above our own, agreeing together on a plan of action. When discord comes, Lord, help us to handle it with empathy and gentleness. Fill us with peace. And let us always take our disagreements to You for redirection, guidance, and confirmation. You alone meld two individuals into one beautiful marriage.

Peace with All

Encourage each other and build each other up, just as you are already doing.... And live peacefully with each other.

1 Thessalonians 5:11, 13 NLT

Oh, Lord, we long to be peace-seekers in this world. We pray for our marriage, that as a couple we would seek peace and pursue it, even in relationships where it is hard to find.

You know the people in our lives, the people we deal with as a married couple. Thank You for providing us with some great relationships—people who encourage us and make it easy to live in peace. We praise You today for them and ask that You would continue to encourage their hearts and bless our fellowship.

And then there are the other relationships. We know You have a purpose for these too. You would not allow the difficult ones if it were not for our good, or perhaps some good we may be able to do in Your name. We also thank You for these people. Help us to encourage them and to build them up. We pray that You would bless them where they are and make them more like Jesus. Give us open hearts toward them, understanding and compassion—eyes to see the way You see. We want to love as You love.

Lord, protect us from the enemy in these relationships. Help us to discern where we must have boundaries even as we pursue peace. Teach us creative ways to seek peace with difficult people and to honor them, even when they reject us. Lord, we must have Your wisdom to know when, where, and how to act. Show us what it means to live at peace and to trust the results to You.

Peace in All Things

Do not be anxious about anything, but in everything, by prayer and petition, with thanksgiving, present your requests to God. And the peace of God, which transcends all understanding, will guard your hearts and your minds in Christ Jesus.

PHILIPPIANS 4:6–7

Precious Father, how we praise You for the promise of Your peace in all things. There is no one else like You; no god, no religion, no system that can truly supply the peace that You give. As Your Word says, it transcends our human understanding. Thank You that Your peace is ours today. Thank You that there is nothing we ever can face in our marriage that is outside the reach of Your peace.

Take away our anxiety and help us to give up control, even of the things we don't know we're worrying about. May Your peace flood our hearts and our minds. May it fill our conversation. May it be our work, our rest, our daily bread. May Your peace go behind us, covering our past. May it be in our midst today, infusing every decision, every moment. And may it go before us into the future, guarding us and protecting us, blanketing whatever comes in Your continued presence and grace.

And Father, make us instruments of Your peace in the world where we live. Where there is fear, let us bring hope. Where there is hatred, let us sow love. Where there are burdens, let us bear them for others, as You taught us. Let our lives be such examples of Your peace that others may see something different in us and be drawn to You—in Jesus' name.

Section
5

The Promise of Faithfulness

Because of the LORD's great love we are not consumed, for his compassions never fail. They are new every morning; great is your faithfulness.

LAMENTATIONS 3:22–23

The marriage covenant itself is a promise to be faithful. Traditional vows include words like "in sickness and in health, for richer, for poorer, till death do us part...." Even in non-traditional ceremonies, the act of marriage is the sealing of a promise, the expression of a desire to be faithful to one person for life. It is a choice—the choice to commit ourselves and to trust our hearts in another's commitment to us.

We have no greater need in marriage—and perhaps no greater challenge—than faithfulness. Temptations are all around, sometimes in obvious forms, but often in the shape of good people and things that can become hazardous if not kept in proper perspective.

Thanks be to God that He is always faithful. We have His faithfulness as our example. But more than that, we also have His faithfulness as a fruit of the Spirit living within us. And we can call on that Spirit to help us any time we are in need.

Relying on God

I have always been mindful of your unfailing love and have lived in reliance on your faithfulness.

<small>PSALM 26:3</small>

Oh, Lord, we thank You today that You are faithful. You never fail—You *cannot* fail. It is not in Your character. We need to be reminded of Your faithful-ness. Like the Psalmist, we want to be always mindful of how much You love us. We want to live in reliance on Your faithfulness to our marriage and in all aspects of our lives.

Forgive us, Lord, for worrying about what could happen. For borrowing trouble. We know that You hold us in Your hand and that we are safe in Your faithful love. You have been so good to us throughout our marriage. You always take care of our needs. Why do we ever question whether You will take care of us?

Help us, Father, to fully rely on Your faithfulness. To truly rest in it. To remember that You are always in control. Nothing is a surprise to You; nothing "slips through the cracks" because there are no cracks in Your love. We choose to turn against fear in the name of Jesus and to trust in Your faithfulness today.

You promise that You will be with us no matter what. You walk beside us through all things. You strengthen and support our marriage. God, help us to follow Your example of faithful love. We pray that You will make us rocks in our marriage; strong, unshakable people of faith our spouses can depend on—a comforting, peaceful presence through any storm.

Together in Faithfulness

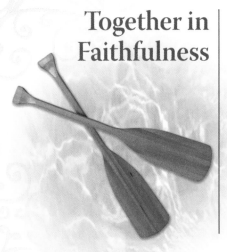

You, Lord, are a compassionate and gracious God, slow to anger, abounding in love and faithfulness.

Psalm 86:15

Father, as we pray Your faithfulness over our marriage, we are aware of our need to be faithful in all things, in all ways. We want to be like You and not only be faithful in big things, but to abound in faithfulness—to overflow with it—in every single area of our marriage. We know faithfulness is a daily choice and that it is only possible through You. We pray that You will fill us afresh with Your power to make that choice. Show us areas that need improvement and give us the grace to make those improvements. Let love and faithfulness define us as Your children and as spouses.

We pray for our marriage today, that You will guard both of us. Bind us together through faithful hearts, minds, and spirits. Lord, there are so many forces we encounter that would pull us away from one another and tempt us to break our promises. Keep us together in Your love. Let us see clearly through the schemes of those who are against us. Even when, and perhaps especially when, something seems good, give us discernment to know if it is from You. Teach us to carefully plan our days and to make right choices about how we spend our time, and with whom we spend it. We pray that the way we use the time we've been given will be pleasing to You and reflect our faithfulness both to You and to one another.

Shielded by Faithfulness

He will cover you with his feathers, and under his wings you will find refuge; his faithfulness will be your shield and rampart.

PSALM 91:4

What a joy it is, Lord, to be covered by Your faithful-ness. We draw close to You today, seeking Your protection, Your armor to shield us. We need and rely on You for shelter and safety.

We pray that You would be our refuge in marriage. That we would look to You and Your faithfulness to hide us and keep us safe from the machinations of those who mean us harm. May we cling to You and Your Word, and always walk in Your ways. You have promised that Your faithfulness is a shield, and we believe it shields our marriage.

Father, sometimes it is so easy to want to step outside of that shield, if only for a moment. The world, it sometimes seems, has no place for faithfulness. No value for honor. Standards seem so low, even among many married couples. But Your thoughts are not our thoughts, and Your ways are not our ways. They are higher. And when we follow You in faithfulness, we are protected from so much heartache and pain. Help us to always remember that truth. To keep it always before us. Your Word truly is a light for our path.

Shield us in Your faithfulness, oh, Lord. Speak to our hearts and show us how to be faithful to one another and to You. And may our faithfulness be a shield for each other and for our family as we walk through life together.

Plans in Perfect Faithfulness

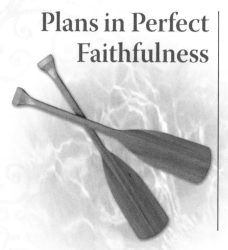

LORD, *you are my God;*
I will exalt you and praise
your name, for in perfect
faithfulness you have done
wonderful things, things
planned long ago.

ISAIAH 25:1

Dear heavenly Father, thank You today for our marriage. Thank You for the life You have given us together, for all of the ways You've been faithful to us, for all of the things You've brought us through. You are such a great and mighty God. Awesome and beautiful are Your ways.

We thank You, also, for where You are taking us in our marriage. We are not the same today as we once were, and You continue to work in our lives. Thank You that in Your perfect faithfulness You have a plan for our life together, plans for a future and a hope. I look forward with anticipation to all You have for us. Thank You that in You we have nothing to dread.

Father, we praise You because Your plans are good. They flow out of Your faithful, loving heart. Thank You that because of Your faithfulness to us we can know that Your plans include joy and peace. Thank You that we are destined not for failure, but victory in Christ Jesus.

Everything You do is wonderful. We commit our plans—all of our ideas and dreams about the future—into Your faithful keeping. In Your wisdom, bring about Your perfect will in us. Help us to be faithful in how we plan our lives, budgets, and future together. Help us not to make selfish plans but to always communicate with one another as we seek to follow Your plan. We trust Your faithfulness and exalt Your name together.

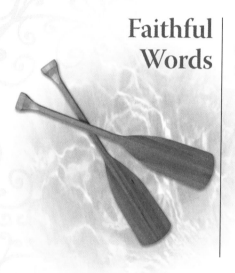

Faithful Words

The righteous will live by their faithfulness to God.

<small>HABAKKUK 2:4 NLT</small>

Oh, Lord, we come to You with hearts that desire to live in faithfulness to one another and to You. We pray that as we grow in our marriage, You will take us deeper and deeper in faithfulness, that You will teach us more and more of what it is.

Today, we pray that You will help us be faithful in our conversation. Sometimes it is tempting to talk about our relationship with others, especially when friends or coworkers are complaining. Help us to remain faithful even in these times, Father, with the words we say and the attitudes we display. May we set an example of a godly marriage, not by giving some false sense of perfection, but by using an honoring tone. Help us faithfully build one another up, focusing on the good qualities we appreciate in one another. Help us use words that build up rather than tear down.

When we do need to talk to someone about a real issue, please give us discernment. We trust You to provide wise counsel when it is needed and to lead us to those who can truly help. In other times, help us to keep the particulars of our relationship between us and You. Help us treat one another faithfully as each of us desires to be treated.

Thank You for the gift of my spouse. Help us to always be faithful in speaking about our relationship and bringing it to You. Bless our marriage and smile upon it, keep our words and our hearts faithful to each other and to You.

Faithfully Made

The LORD will work out his plans for my life— for your faithful love, O LORD, endures forever. Don't abandon me, for you made me.

PSALM 138:8 NLT

God, You made us the way we are. You know what makes us laugh, what makes us angry, what fuels our frustration, what gives us hope. Thank You for making us such unique individuals. You made us according to Your pattern and have been faithful in giving us the gifts and characteristics we need in marriage with each other. Thank You for giving us such wonderful potential to be faithful to our Creator and to each other.

Lord, work out Your plans for us by using our individual strengths. Help us to follow the path You have set before us, being faithful to who we are as Your children. Your workmanship is marvelous. Help us to identify and appreciate the special quirks, talents, and skills You have bestowed upon us. Help us to use those personality traits to fill in for the other's weaknesses, to build each other up, to form two perfectly matched pieces in one seamless marriage.

Your love is faithful, oh, Lord. You molded us into being, but that was just the beginning. You never abandon us. Your hand guides us. Your love sets the example for our marriage. Without You we are just two quirky individuals. With You we have a harmonious union. Thank You for letting us be who we are and so much more. Through You we are more than the sum of our parts. Bless our uniqueness and be faithful to us even as we build our marriage in Your name.

Section
6

The Promise of a Full Life

*Jesus answered, "I am the way
and the truth and the life.
No one comes to the Father
except through me."*

Jesus came not only to show us how to live, but to actually *live fully*. The Bible is brimming with gifts God has given us—verses with guidelines to follow, protections, provisions, and encouragement on how to have a successful married life. But the greatest gift God ever gave a married couple is the gift of His Son, who *is* life.

Having a marriage that honors Him is not something we produce on our own by acting spiritual. While the fruits of a marriage that's alive in Christ may be visible to others, life is not about something outward. It's not about how hard we work or what we do so much as it is about who we are in Jesus, and who we allow Him to be in us. When we allow Him full reign in our lives, our lives overflow with gratitude, generosity, and contentment.

Jesus is life and everything that means life—and a marriage that's alive is a marriage full of Jesus. He lives daily, fully in us.

Fullness of Life

I have come that they may have life, and have it to the full.

John 10:10

Abundant life. Life to the full. Thank You, Jesus, that You came to give us life—that You made life possible. Because of You no one can steal or kill or destroy my marriage. It belongs to You. We belong to You and we choose the life You died on the cross to give us.

We pray the abundance of Your life over our marriage today. Because of You our life together can be full, not empty or shallow. As Your children we have a purpose. You have a plan for us. We do not live for ourselves, but for You.

Thank You that we are not destined for mediocrity, but for fullness of life. You make our relationships deep and meaningful. You make our work something valuable. You direct our steps, our conversations, our plans. You make our home a place of peace and joy, and not just a landing place between activities. You hold our future and give us hope.

We pray protection over our marriage, that You would guard us from the temptations that steal joy or limit our enjoyment of each other. Every good thing You have planned for our life together, we claim today as Your children. May those who oppose You never steal even a minute from us again. We don't want to miss a single moment of the life You want to live in us and through us. You, Jesus, bring to us a fullness of life. Thank You.

Really Live

I command you today:
Love GOD, your God.
Walk in his ways. Keep his
commandments, regulations,
and rules so that you
will live, really live, live
exuberantly, blessed
by GOD, your God.

DEUTERONOMY 30:16 MSG

Father, as we pray the promise of a full life over our marriage today, we are keenly aware that to really live is a choice. We're committing to You now that we choose Your life and Your blessing in our marriage. We want to live exuberantly together and to be blessed by God.

We pray for one another today, that You will give the grace that is needed to choose Your path in every moment. No matter what comes into our day, help us both to see clearly the choice to embrace the God-given life You've offered us. We pray that You will help us to celebrate this day and every day, to keep our love fresh and not allow our marriage to become boring or trying.

Thank You that we can live together with a fullness of joy. Thank You for the milestones we can mark together—for all of the ways You allow us to grow in love. You are our life! May we always choose the path that leads us closer to You and fills our lives with good things. There are so many blessings to count. Help us to embrace every opportunity to live, really live for You.

Prosperity and Honor

He who pursues righteousness and love finds life, prosperity and honor.

PROVERBS 21:21

We are so thankful for Your promises today, God. It fills our hearts with gratitude to know that You are faithful, that You grant us peace and blessing, and that You are always with us. You are our Maker and our Sustainer. Thank You that You are the life in our marriage, bringing us prosperity and honor.

We know that Your definitions are not always the same as ours. While You may choose to grant prosperity and honor in outward ways, the gifts of the Kingdom are always deeper than the surface. So today, as we commit to You to pursue righteousness and love in our marriage, we receive Your fullness of life down deep in our souls. We receive spiritual prosperity. We receive spiritual honor.

Thank You for fullness of life. Thank You that through Jesus we can have joy—true joy—in any circumstance. Thank You for a prosperity that goes beyond "things" and an honor that goes beyond pride. Thank You for Your peace. There is nothing greater we could ever ask for, in heaven or earth. This is life—knowing You and living in Your presence.

Thank You for prospering and honoring our marriage. May we look to You every day for our daily bread. May we bring honor to Your name through our marriage. Thank You for choosing us and making our lives worth living.

A Life of Wisdom

Know also that wisdom is like honey for you: If you find it, there is a future hope for you, and your hope will not be cut off.

<small>PROVERBS 24:14</small>

What a treasure Your wisdom is to us, Father. Thank You for calling us and leading us in Your wisdom. Thank You that You walk with us in fullness of life. Please keep us near You and give us the wisdom to seek You always, filling us with hope as we struggle with the day-to-day ups and downs of marriage.

Lord, we see so many marriages around us crumbling, either in divorce, unfaithfulness, or simply in disrespect and unhappiness. Your Word is true where it says that broad is the road that leads to destruction. It is hard not to give in sometimes, to not be one of the crowd. But as we pray for our marriage, we are reminded that following the crowd is not really easier. In the long run it leads to so much destruction in people's lives—we've seen it over and over again. Help us to persistently resist.

May our marriage flourish from following Your wisdom. Oh, God, give us the strength we need in our individual characters to hold fast to what is good and right; to cling to Your leading; to hold on tightly to one another and truly love and trust one another. Help us, Lord, in all of the little and big choices we make, and guide us when we encounter trouble or temptation. May we continue to be one of those rare couples who truly find life and wisdom in You.

All Your Might

Whatever your hand finds to do, do it with all your might.

ECCLESIASTES 9:10

Jesus, we pray that we would lose ourselves in You as we work together for our future. We pray that our "wants" would decrease that You may increase. May we let go of all of our claims and ideas about what life should be, our expectations and entitlements. Our marriage is worth investing everything we are, worth following wherever You may lead. Help us to guard our marriage with all our might.

Make us servants, oh, Lord, like You were when You were on the earth. Help us live our lives for the good of one other in our marriage. We don't want to elevate ourselves, but to build a marriage that is worthy of You. We want to reflect Your love in our marriage, our home, our jobs, our community. We want You to look at our lives and see an offering that pleases You, that blesses Your heart. We want to follow You with everything we have, using all our resources for Your glory.

Show us what it means to live our lives for Your sake. May we not be unnecessary martyrs, or try to manufacture spiritual behavior, but may we follow as You lead us, holding nothing back. You are our example. You laid down Your life that we may live. Today, we're giving our marriage to You to use however You will. Strip us bare of anything that's not of God. Help us to work at our marriage with all of our might.

Life of Contentment

I am not saying this because I am in need, for I have learned to be content whatever the circumstances.

PHILIPPIANS 4:11

Father, thank You for giving us everything we need. We are totally fulfilled in You. On days when we start wondering what it would be like to have more, bigger, better, remind us of all the blessings You have provided. Thank You for our life together, for the amazing blessing of marriage.

We pray the promise of contentment over our marriage today. You are everything to us; in You we find all that we need.

Whether we have much or little, may You bring the freshness of Your spirit to us, renewing us in Your mighty power. Breathe Your life into us, that we may live and move and have our contentment in You. Help us to appreciate the little things in every day—all of the kindnesses You show us—to be satisfied with what You provide. We know this is the way to live life to the fullest.

As we are filled with more and more contentment in our marriage, let us minister a spirit of peace into the lives of others, that they may see Your provision. May we be happy with where You have placed us and with the gift of each other. May our marriage display the great blessing of Your contentment. May we find peace with our circumstances, be they great or small.

Full of Happiness

*Give me happiness,
O Lord, for I give myself
to you. O Lord, you are so
good, so ready to forgive,
so full of unfailing love for
all who ask for your help.*

PSALM 86:4–5 NLT

Wow, God, You are so amazing. You love us no matter what. You tell us to be full of joy and happiness. That is what we are trying to do. Help us to give our worry, anxiety, doubt, and negative attitudes to You so we can fill our lives with the good things You have for us.

Fill us up with so much joy in Your presence that everyone who sees our marriage wants to get close to You to experience the same level of happiness. Open our hearts to the beauty of each day, the joy of companionship, the fullness of love. We give our lives to You. We give our marriage to You. Use us to bring joy to others.

God, You are the source of happiness in our marriage. Continue to bless us with affection for each other. Help our lives to echo with laughter and good-natured fun. Help us to find the silver lining in every trial and offer forgiveness for every wrong. God, we want the deep, abiding joy that we can only receive from You. We ask for Your help in keeping love and happiness in our marriage even during seasons that aren't very fun. We trust You, God, to help us choose joy. Thank You for showing us how to live life fully, experiencing Your joy every day.

Section
7

The Promise of Grace

*From the fullness of his grace we have
all received one blessing after another.*

JOHN 1:16

Grace. Like love, it's a word that gets tossed around a lot. In fact, it's so familiar that many may take it for granted. It sounds nice and vaguely like something we need in our lives. But what is grace, really?

For the Christian, there is nothing more important than grace. It is central to everything we believe. It's what saves us in the first place, and what we depend on as we live out our lives—the unmerited favor of God. It is the idea that we can do nothing, good or bad, to change the way God feels about us. He is for us. He loves us. And that is final.

Such grace has transformative power in marriage. Because of the grace God pours out on us, we are free to extend His grace to our spouses and our families. And His grace is enough for any need. We can call on His grace at any time. It is there for our marriage no matter what. God's supply of grace toward us is endless; His ocean never runs dry.

Full of Grace

Be wise in the way you act toward outsiders; make the most of every opportunity. Let your conversation be always full of grace, seasoned with salt, so that you may know how to answer everyone.

Colossians 4:5–6

Thank You, Jesus, that You came to dwell among us as the embodiment of grace. Thank You that Your heart toward us is grace; that You never tire of showing us grace; that Your supply of grace never runs out. We need Your grace in our marriage today.

We pray that You will help us represent You well as we

display our marriage to the outside world. May we be patient and kind, expecting the best and giving grace when others are not at their best. Especially with one another, may we always be ready to show grace. When hormones are flaring or egos are wounded, may we remember that these moments are temporary. May we show the grace to one another that we so desperately need in return.

Help us, Father, to hold our tongues when times are difficult. Sometimes that requires a lot of grace—the grace to be self-controlled. The grace not to retaliate, not to make things worse with our words. We trust You to give us the grace we need in this area, and in all areas of our life together.

Jesus, when we talk to others, let us speak with grace and wisdom. Give us the words to speak that reflect Your grace to everyone we meet.

All Grace at All Times

God is able to make all grace abound to you, so that in all things at all times, having all that you need, you will abound in every good work.

2 CORINTHIANS 9:8

Dear God, thank You so much for Your grace in our marriage. Thank You that through Your grace You brought us together as husband and wife, in Your grace You bless and keep us now, and that by Your grace You hold our future in Your hands. Nothing happens without Your grace.

Thank You that we have access to Your grace at all times. Please help us remember that it is there and it is all we need to live the Christian life in a way that brings honor and glory to You. Even when times are tough, when we are tired or fed up, You can cover us in grace. We don't have to necessarily feel grace-full to extend grace. We can trust You to use it for good.

Lord, we need Your grace. We know You have plans for us, good works You intend us to do. May we have the grace to see Your will and where You are working. Help us to have grace under pressure and equip us to carry out Your will. Whether it is at home, work, church, in the community, or out in the far reaches of the world, we know there is nothing outside the limits of Your grace. You Word says all grace at all times for all that we need. That covers any situation we can ever face! We call upon You for that all-encompassing grace today, and receive all we need for our marriage.

Grace for Mistakes

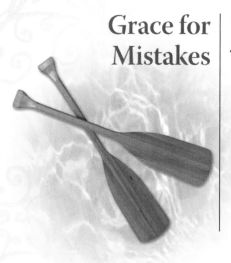

Generous in love—God, give grace! Huge in mercy—wipe out my bad record.

PSALM 51:1 MSG

Father, sometimes we fool ourselves into thinking that we can have a perfect marriage. Then when disappointments come, we get frustrated or angry because the perfection has been shattered. And that disappointment can snowball into real problems.

Father, make our home a place where we allow each other to make mistakes. Make ours a grace-based home where even though things may not be perfect, we offer grace and understanding. Remind us that we get to live with the love of our lives. We chose each other. On days when mistakes are made, help us realize that our spouse is not our enemy. When we lose our cool, help us to go back to our mate and ask for forgiveness. Mistakes are part of life and growth. Let us never exploit our spouse's mistakes as a reason to withhold love. Use our differences, vulnerabilities, and weaknesses to bind us together and bring us more fully into dependence on Your grace.

When we make mistakes, Father, give us grace. Take away our pride, bitterness, foolishness, or whatever it is that makes us pull away from each other. Give us the grace to reach out in love. To be vulnerable and open. Help us to admit our wrongs, to ask each other for forgiveness, to extend grace. Through You we can get past differences. With You by our side we can go beyond the illusion of a perfect marriage and grow our marriage into one full of grace, mercy, and love.

His Grace Is Sufficient

He said to me, "My grace is sufficient for you, for my power is made perfect in weakness." Therefore I will boast all the more gladly about my weaknesses, so that Christ's power may rest on me. That is why, for Christ's sake, I delight in weaknesses, in insults, in hardships, in persecutions, in difficulties. For when I am weak, then I am strong.

2 Corinthians 12:9–10

How sweet the sound of Your grace is to us, oh, Lord. It's truly amazing that You could save wretches like us. As we pray Your grace over our marriage, we see our many needs, our many weaknesses, the many places in our own hearts and lives where we require Your strength. We thank You that Your grace is sufficient for all of these things.

Lord, You know our hearts. You know our potential for good as well as the darkness that lies within us. You know the weaknesses, insults, hardships, persecutions, and difficulties we are facing. How we long to be able to delight in those things for Your sake. In order for that to happen, however, we need a move of Your grace in our marriage, a heart of forgiveness for each other.

Please bring a fresh filling of Your grace in our lives today. Because of Your grace we are more than the sum of our failures. You have promised that our weaknesses can actually be transformed into trophies of Your grace. Oh, Lord, let it be so in our marriage today. When we make a mess help us to forgive one another; bathe us in Your grace. Show us the way to redemption. Help us to offer forgiveness to each other and ourselves. All we have to offer You is our weakness, but we give it to You now. Take it and use it to make our marriage strong.

Overcoming Temptation

We do not have a high priest who is unable to sympathize with our weaknesses, but we have one who has been tempted in every way, just as we are—yet was without sin. Let us then approach the throne of grace with confidence, so that we may receive mercy and find grace to help us in our time of need.

HEBREWS 4:15–16

We worship You, Jesus, our God and our King. How blessed we are that You understand our human condition. That You see us and sympathize with us. But, You have not left us helpless in sin. You also supply us the power we need to overcome our temptations.

Thank You that we may come to You in prayer for our marriage and have confidence that You will help us and give us grace and mercy when we are faced with tempting situations. We thank You also that You intercede for us and that in Your grace You are always looking out for our marriage.

Father, just as Your heart toward us is grace, we pray that You will give us hearts of grace in our marriage. May we always be a safe place for one another. May we be so loving and kind toward one another—so gracious—that we may approach each other with confidence. May we be each other's helper, always there for one another in times of need. Help us also to be merciful in our interactions. Help us follow Your example, showing grace to one another as Christ has shown grace to His bride, the Church, laying down our lives for the other's good.

As we walk in Your grace, let it be a living, dynamic force between us that transforms our marriage. Lead us deeper and deeper into You, that we may share Your grace with the world.

Grace to the Humble

God opposes the proud but gives grace to the humble.

JAMES 4:6

Dear God, I pray for humility in my marriage. May we never be proud, haughty, or rude with one another. Because of Your grace we can overcome the temptation to be arrogant, to speak and act unkindly. Please give us the grace to be humble.

Because of Your grace at work in us we can speak words of wisdom, words that heal rather than tear down. I pray for understanding between us, for open hearts. I pray today that neither of us will respond in anger when we are disappointed, but that we will use soft voices with one another. May we be mindful that we are dust. That anything we are or have comes from You.

Father, help us to move in humility throughout the day, that Your grace may rest on us. Help us not to seek to be served, but to serve one another in love. Give us that extra endurance we need, the extra patience with each other to live together gracefully. When we make mistakes or are not at our best, let grace abound in our relationship all the more.

Lord, as I pray grace over my marriage I see the opportunity You have given me to show grace to my partner. The marriage relationship really is a daily forum for grace—a place it is so needed, a place You can be glorified over all. This is my heart's cry today, that You will make me a person of grace, and fill my marriage with grace. Help me to be humble, that You may extend more and more grace in my marriage through me.

Our Gracious Lord

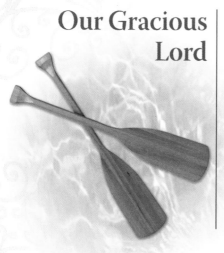

The LORD longs to be gracious to you; he rises to show you compassion. For the LORD is a God of justice. Blessed are all who wait for him!

ISAIAH 30:18

When we grasp a hold of Your promises, Lord, it changes our lives. You have freely given us so much good, so much beauty and life in our marriage. And the idea that You long to give us grace—Your favor, Your unconditional love—overwhelms us, motivates us, and compels us to bow our hearts before You. You are so generous, so loving and kind.

Thank You for the compassion You show us. Help us to show that same compassion to each other. We wait to see Your grace, Your wisdom, Your power displayed in our marriage, and we know that we are blessed as we wait for You.

Father, may Your grace fall on us—on every aspect of our lives together. May every decision we make, from the great to the small, be immersed in it. May our home be filled with Your grace so that everyone who enters may sense Your presence. May our conversation, our activities, our habits, our finances, our physical and emotional relationship—everything about our marriage—be covered in grace. May it be more than just a pretty word, but a way of life for us. May we never fall into a system of trying to earn Your favor or that of one another, but cling to Your grace alone. Father, fulfill Your longing to be gracious to us. We receive it as Your gift—and the sustenance of our marriage—today.

Section 8

The Promise of Provision

*My God will meet all your needs
according to his glorious riches
in Christ Jesus.*

PHILIPPIANS 4:19

In Romans 8:14 the apostle Paul instructs us to come to God as His adopted children and to call Him not only "Father," but "Abba," which basically means "Daddy." This is a good starting place when we consider the promise of His provision for us in marriage. We have a heavenly Father whose heart toward us is that of a loving, doting parent. A parent who desires only our good. A parent who watches over our lives as we might bend over a newborn child, with tender longing. A Father who wants to be so much more to us than an authority figure, but also our friend, our protector, our provider, our biggest fan. *Daddy.*

Pair this kind of heart with the unlimited resources of an infinite God. He owns everything in the universe. He is all-powerful. All-seeing and knowing. There's not a need we have in our marriage that He is unable to provide. He meets them all if we only ask.

Our Provider

I was young and now I am old, yet I have never seen the righteous forsaken or their children begging bread.

PSALM 37:25

Thank You, Father, that in these uncertain times we can trust in Your promise of provision. It is easy to fear when we look around us, but today we choose to look to You. You do not forsake Your children. Your Word says You will provide for us in every way, and we come to You now claiming that promise for our marriage. Be our provider—our Jehovah Jireh—as we look to You for all of our needs.

Father, You know our bills. You know what it takes for us to live. Give us wisdom as we use the resources You provide for us. Help us see what is necessary and right for us to keep in our budget and what we might be able to cut in order to save. Give us hearts that are willing to sacrifice material things in order to spiritually live. Help us to depend on You for daily bread. We know You will never fail us.

As we trust in You for all of our needs, may we also look to the needs of others. Help us not to turn away when there is something we can do. Like You, Jesus, may we relieve suffering where we see it in any form as much as we are able. Help us hold our material blessings loosely and see them as tools to bless others, candles we can use to light up Your world.

How Much More

Which of you, if his son asks for bread, will give him a stone? Or if he asks for a fish, will give him a snake? If you, then, though you are evil, know how to give good gifts to your children, how much more will your Father in heaven give good gifts to those who ask him!

MATTHEW 7:9–11

Heavenly Father, we want to know You as our Abba Father. As we pray the promise of Your provision over our marriage, teach us to look to You as Abba. To see You as the loving, caring, kind, tender "Daddy" sort of protector and provider that You truly are. Help us draw close to Your heart and allow You to love and provide for us so much more than any human parent ever could.

We confess that sometimes we are tempted to doubt Your provision. We know with our heads that the Bible says You give good gifts, but our hearts need help believing it—and receiving it—in our marriage. Sometimes we feel we are asking too much of You, that You've given us enough and must tire of hearing all of our requests. But this not what Your Word says about Your character at all. We believe Your Word; Lord, help our unbelief. Forgive us.

You have given us so many good gifts and for those we are thankful. Father, we are in need of more in our marriage. More love, more grace, more transparency, more of You in our lives. We recognize that all good things flow from You, and we are seeking all the good that You are. Flood our marriage with an outpouring of Your Spirit that we may know You and love You—and love one another—so much more.

Everything to Enjoy

Hope in God, who richly provides us with everything for our enjoyment.

1 TIMOTHY 6:17

What a great God You are, Lord. Knowing that You richly provide for our marriage gives us hope. We pray that we would look for Your fingerprints on all of the things we enjoy. You are everywhere, and Your loving provision for us is so apparent if only we take the time to see it.

Thank You for the world You made. For sunshine on our faces. Thank You for the wind and the blue sky and for stars.

Thank You for fun. For creativity, beauty. Thank You for work time and play time. For family and friends. Thank You for our daily bread, and for the ways You nourish us both physically and spiritually. Thank You for a place to live, for life and for love.

Lord, may we never separate things in our marriage into categories of spiritual and unspiritual. Your Word says You richly provide *everything* for us to enjoy—everything we need, not just for existence, but for enjoyment! What a wonderful world that opens up for us in our lives, and in our relationship. Whether it be chocolate, a favorite song, a favorite place, a sunset, or a kiss, help us to recognize all of the good things that flow to us from You.

Teach us, oh, Lord, to enjoy the things You have for us, the things that lead to life and health and peace. May we walk in contentment, enjoying all You have provided.

No Good Thing

For the LORD God is a sun and shield; the LORD bestows favor and honor; no good thing does he withhold from those whose walk is blameless.

PSALM 84:11

Lord, we are on our knees before You. Be the sun and shield of our marriage. Grant us Your favor and honor, and by Your Spirit help us to walk blamelessly before You all of our days.

Sometimes we have a skewed view of Your character. A limited view. Though we know better, we often buy into the lie of the world, that You may keep good things from us because we don't deserve them. Or worse yet, because You are powerful and You can, You keep things from us.

This promise—that You withhold no good thing from us—challenges us. It brings us back to the truth of Your all-consuming love and kindness. It opens our hearts to the possibility—the reality—that You give us good things in our marriage. That You will continue to give them. No good thing will You withhold.

We pray this promise over our marriage and ask for all of the good things You want to give. For all of the things we need in our marriage: Your blessing, intimacy with You and with each other, peace in our hearts and home, unshakable faith—and faithfulness to one another and You in all things. We need Your love to flow between us and outward from us to, in turn, give good things to others. Provide for us, Lord, that we may glorify You in our marriage. We trust Your heart to withhold from us no good thing.

According to His Will

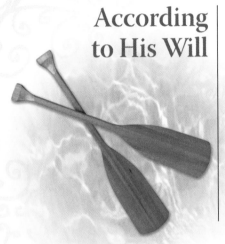

This is the confidence we have in approaching God: that if we ask anything according to his will, he hears us. And if we know that he hears us— whatever we ask—we know that we have what we asked of him.

1 JOHN 5:14–15

Our Abba Father, we praise You today for who You are. Thank You that we can approach You in prayer with confidence that You hear us. Thank You that nothing can thwart Your ultimate will for us. We give You thanks and praise for all You have provided for us in our marriage.

Husband: Lord, You know my heart and the things I desire in my relationship with my wife. You know the needs I have and how to meet them. You know my dreams for our future and the material and eternal things I want to pursue. You know what I desire.

But, Father, I don't want to drive my own agenda. I desire Your will above all my own ideas and plans. Right now, I submit my will to Yours. I ask these things according to Your will, meaning that if they are Your will, let them come to pass in Your time. And if they are not Your will, keep them from us, that we may receive Your higher good.

Wife: Father, I agree with my husband's prayer. I know that You know me inside and out as well, and You are acquainted with all of my ways. You know everything that my heart desires.

In this moment, I'm submitting my will to Yours as well. I give my desires over to Your keeping, asking for them to be fulfilled only according to Your will. I pray that You would align our hearts so closely with Yours that we may learn Your will and desire it.

Everything We Need

His divine power has given us everything we need for life and godliness through our knowledge of him who called us by his own glory and goodness.

2 PETER 1:3

Father, there are times in our marriage when the Christian life seems impossible to live. We get so frustrated we think of giving up, and then we remember Your promises to provide everything we need. We're standing firm on Your promises today. We're calling upon Your divine power to provide exactly what we need to live a godly life.

Lord, You know our needs better than we do. Help us be content with much or with little, trusting You for everything. May we use what You have given us to honor You and bless others.

We pray for one another, that You may grant us mercy. Forgive us where we have failed You. Help us to treat one another as You would, even when it is hard. Break through our defenses, that we may access Your power and accept Your grace. Jesus, it is our knowledge of Your goodness that fuels life and godliness, that brings about the great contentment in any relationship. Thank You for giving us everything we need to power a great marriage.

Help us to be thankful when You withhold harmful things from us, things that would send us down the wrong path, remembering that through You we have the essentials covered. Thank You, Lord, that You hold us together through thick and thin. Even when we don't feel like it, we're trusting the truth of the promise that Your divine power has given us everything we need for life and godliness in our marriage.

Provision in Tough Times

God is good, a hiding place in tough times. He recognizes and welcomes anyone looking for help, no matter how desperate the trouble.

Nahum 1:7 msg

Lord, thank You for being our safe place, our Provider. When things are tough, when we don't know when the next check is coming or how we are going to make ends meet, help us to rely on You. Help us to put all our trust in You. Sometimes things make no sense in our world, but we know that You have a plan that makes divine sense.

You say that You welcome anyone looking for help, Lord. That is us. We need You to intervene in our marriage and show us the way. Smooth out the path before us. Give us the persistence and strength we'll need to get through desperate times. Oh, Lord, You always have just what we need, right when we need it. Sometimes we worry about the timing or the logistics. But there is no need. Soothe our worries, Lord. Calm our fears.

In tough times, Lord, we tend to take our stress out on each other. Give us patience. Bring us peace. You are in control of everything in our marriage. Help us to remember that You are good—in the good times and the bad, the full times and the lean. You are the ultimate Provider. Provide us with compassion and understanding toward each other. We want to be strong together, and we know that through You we can be.

Thank You for all You provide, for the answers to prayers big and small. Thank You for peace and grace and tolerance. Thank You for welcoming arms.

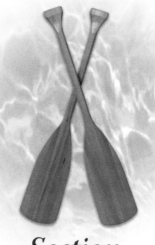

Section **9**

The Promise of Love

*[The] Lord, the great and awesome
God...keeps his covenant of love with all
who love him and obey his commands.*

DANIEL 9:4

Love is not optional with God. It is a promise, a covenant He has made with us as His children. Just as He cannot be unfaithful, He cannot withhold His love. It's just not in His character.

In marriage, this is a dual comfort. First, He loves us. Whether our spouse loves us or not, God loves us. Whether we're beautiful, lovable, deserving, or not, He loves us. Whether we feel like it or not, God loves us. Nothing can take that away from us, and nothing can separate us from His love. It is a constant, faithful, and steady truth we can cling to in a world that is always changing.

The second comfort we can derive from His love in marriage is that because He keeps His promise to love us, we can keep our promise to love our husband or wife. Whether our spouse loves us or not, we can love. Whether our spouse is beautiful, loving, deserving, or not, we can love. Whether we feel like it or not, we can choose to love, because God first loved us.

Choose Love

Now these three remain: faith, hope and love. But the greatest of these is love.

1 CORINTHIANS 13:13

We are so blessed that You love us, Lord. It's unfathomable, really, that You would choose to love us and desire a relationship with us. Being loved by You changes our lives. It compels us to want to live for You and to love others the way that You love. Lead us, oh, Lord, to choose love daily on behalf of our marriage. Guide us in Your unfailing love.

As we seek to choose love, Lord, help us to follow Your example. May we always act in love, and not out of a selfish motivation. Give us hearts that look out for the needs of each other above our own needs. Help us to be patient and kind, never arrogant or boastful or rude. Give us endurance. As we follow Your lead, help us lay down our lives for each other, our best friend.

Father, You know that sometimes it is hard for us to be loving. We pray today that You will help us to see our relationship as Your design, and to follow Your example in our marriage. Give us spirits that are humble. Help us be encouragers to each other, and not hindrances. As we seek You together, lead us into all things good. Thank You for choosing to love us. And help us to always choose love.

Unquenchable Love

You've captured my heart....
You looked at me,
and I fell in love.
One look my
way and I was
hopelessly in love!

SONG OF SOLOMON 4:9–10 MSG

Dear Jesus, thank You for our love. Thank You for giving us an attraction for each other that grew into admiration, respect, and commitment. Traditional marriage vows include the phrase "with my body, I thee worship." Help us to love each other with that kind of intensity. To be so hopelessly in love that we desire each other with our hearts, our minds, and our bodies.

Remind us of the things that drew us together, of how we longed for each other, how just a look could make us tremble, and how we wanted to discuss everything with each other. Daily frustrations intrude on our love and make us forget that desire. Jesus, renew our love moment by moment. Refresh our desire touch by touch. Help us to fall in love with each other over and over again.

Jesus, bind us together with a love so strong that the world cannot break it. Help us to use our emotions, words, and bodies to shower love on each other. Bless all aspects of our marriage. Plant within us a desire to be together, to put our marriage above all other relationships, to deeply, truly enjoy being husband and wife. Build our love for each other to the point where we crave time together. Your Word says that "many waters cannot quench love" (Song of Songs 8:7). Make our love unquenchable.

Love One Another

Love one another as if your lives depended on it.

1 Peter 1:22 MSG

What joy it brings our hearts to know that You take delight in us, oh, Lord. We don't understand it, but Your Word promises it is true, and we trust in Your Word. Thank You also that You are with us, that You help us to take delight in each other.

As we pray Your love into, over, beneath, behind, and throughout our marriage, we want to focus today on loving each other like our lives depended on it. Your Word says to love with a pure heart, to love fiercely. Help us to do that. In a world that can package evil in glamour, we are in need of purity and strong self-control in our marriage.

Quiet our hearts before You, Lord. May we be still and know that You are God. May we draw so close to You that we can hear Your heartbeat and let it set the tempo for our love. Show us Your will for the day, Your plans, regardless of what the calendar says. And as we go out into the day, help us to keep our connection to each other and to You at the forefront.

At the end of the day, please bring us home safely to one another and let us know that we have honored You as good and faithful servants, that we have loved with every ounce of our energy. May Your love reign in our hearts and in our marriage and our home.

No Greater Love

My command is this: Love each other as I have loved you. Greater love has no one than this, that he lay down his life for his friends.

JOHN 15:12–13

Jesus, Your command is clear. It's the greatest challenge of a Christian marriage, and I'm sure it is also the greatest reward. *Love. Love each other as I have loved you.*

Sometimes we think we are pretty good at loving, at least we try to do a lot of the right things. But as we pray this promise over our marriage today, it comes so clear that Your kind of love is different than ours. It demands more than "a lot of the right things." It demands everything. You gave Your life for us, and Your kind of love demands that we lay down our lives for each other.

How can we do that? It seems impossible. You know that my spouse can be difficult sometimes. And if we are honest, we have to admit neither of us are the easiest people to love. It is only by Your power working in us that we can begin to love as You love.

Oh, Jesus, we want to be like You in our marriage relationship—to love one another as You love. To lay down our very lives. We know this is not possible in ourselves. We are too selfish, too human. But through You we can overcome the sinful nature. We can live a radical love like You did, even when it required Your life. Speak to our hearts, Lord Jesus. Show us what it means to lay down our lives for one another, and give us the grace to do it.

His Ways Are Loving

All the ways of the LORD are loving and faithful for those who keep the demands of his covenant.

PSALM 25:10

Dear heavenly Father, it astounds us that You are loving and faithful in all of Your ways. Your Word says that You are not a man; Your ways are not our ways. How true that is, especially when it comes to love.

How we long to be loving and faithful in all of our ways in this marriage. Please help us, dear Father. Examine our ways.

From the small details to the big things, remove those ways that are not loving and faithful. Create in us a clean heart and renew a right spirit within us, that we may begin to love one another as You first loved us.

We give You our reasons—excuses really—for not loving. Held up in light of the cross, they no longer make sense. Today, we want to follow You in our marriage. Help us to stop complaining, to stop finding excuses. May we quit focusing only on our own selfish needs, that we may be free to love one another— to live the love You so lavishly pour out on us.

We know we cannot do this without Your Spirit here to guide us. So, Father, we invite You into our marriage today. Lead us into all truth, even if the truth about our ability to love is painful. Your Word says the wounds of a friend bring healing, and we pray that You will wound our pride if necessary, in order to bring healing to our marriage. Thank You, Father, for demonstrating for us how to be faithful and loving.

Belonging to Each Other

My lover is mine and I am his....
His banner over me is love.

SONG OF SONGS 2:16, 4

Father, how sweet it is to be loved by You. To belong to You. To live under Your shelter of love. I pray today that my marriage would be a reflection of this perfect loving relationship— belonging, protecting, giving, and receiving.

Husband: I pray for my wife, that she will know she always belongs with me and that I belong to her. Help me to give freely of my love—to lavish it on her—and to also gracefully receive the love she has for me and show her my appreciation.

Father, help me to be a loving protector. As You set Your love over us to guard us, may I protect my wife in the same way. May I be a man my wife can trust in, a husband she can run to for safety. May I never put my own interests before hers. Give me courage to protect her above all others in my life.

Wife: Lord, I pray for my husband. May he feel a sense of belonging with me; may I be a strong tower where he can be safe. May he know that he is secure in my love and that no one could ever take his place. Help me to be extravagant in my love toward him, to treat him as the most special man on earth, because he is. Thank You for the gift You have given me in him.

I pray Your protection over our marriage, and that You will help me to dwell under my husband's protection. Keep us always under Your banner of love.

Nothing Can Separate Us

Who shall separate us from the love of Christ? Shall trouble or hardship or persecution or famine or nakedness or danger or sword?... No, in all these things we are more than conquerors through him who loved us. For I am convinced that neither death nor life, neither angels nor demons, neither the present nor the future...nor anything else in all creation, will be able to separate us from the love of God that is in Christ Jesus our Lord.

Romans 8:35, 37–39

Dear gracious, loving God, our hearts are full as we ponder Your love—a love we can never comprehend. A love that reaches out to us and holds us in a mystical union with our divine God. Beyond human understanding, and yet as close and familiar to us as our own breath.

How we thank You and praise You that nothing can separate us from Your love, no matter what. We could name the worst thing that could possibly happen to us and still Your love would be there, steadfast and sure. What a comfort this is as we walk through life together.

We pray this same kind of love—Your faithful love—over our marriage. Give us a huge measure of Your grace. Let us love each other as You love. Let us be so strong, so secure in Your love that we are able to extend that love throughout our married life. Help us to lay down our lives for each other. To let nothing on earth separate us.

Regardless of what hardships come our way, make us more than conquerors through Jesus, who loves us. How powerful is that love that overcame even death. We praise You for it, Jesus, and take You as our example. May all of yesterday, today, and whatever happens in our marriage in the future be bathed in Your love.

*F*ather, we trust in all of Your promises
for our marriage. As You lead us, let us renew
our promise to love and honor each other
under Your covenant. We receive from You
everything we need to keep these promises,
and we thank You and praise You for Your
continued work in our marriage. Amen.